From the Island

Judith Small

Black Oyster Press, San Francisco, California
and Chicago, Illinois
Copyright © 1982 by Judith Small
All rights reserved.

ISBN: 0-9605966-1-5

Book design and images by Debbie Costello

Address all inquiry to:
Debbie Costello
P.O. Box 8550
Chicago, Illinois 60680

For my mother and her mother, and for Bob

"... though it be a maxim in the schools *that there is no love of a thing unknown,* yet I have found that things unknown have a secret influence on the soul, and like the centre of the earth unseen violently attract it. We love we know not what, and therefore everything allures us. As iron at a distance is drawn by the loadstone, there being some invisible communication between them, so is there in us a world of love to somewhat, though we know not what in the world that should be."

— Thomas Traherne

Dream of the dance of approach

     "Do not wonder that you have been chosen. This will be difficult until you remember you have always been a dancer."

     Across the floor as across a polished sea I am drawn.

     "In the beginning," she tells me, "you must show fear in every movement. In each wrist, almost invisibly, one bone will tremble like a wren cupped in your palm. Slowly the fear will leave your body and your arms will know by the way they swing, by the way they make an arch above your head and invite you to walk through.

     "This is a slow dance. For many hours you will hear drums, and then a needle slipping through the rhythm in the shape of a flute. You will be glad for your feather headdress and your apricot skirt, above all you will discover your legs are bare and can carry you anywhere.

     "As night comes, though you leap higher fear will return with muffled oars. You cannot hesitate. In the dark of your heart where the pilings crumble and rats go quietly about their business, sharpen your teeth. If needed, you will remember.

     "You will remember, when night is over and each face becomes finally visible, their simplest names: wolf, deer, bear, horse. They have been waiting a long time. Do you know the song you learned in the forest or even before, in the sea? You will sing in a clear voice."

"All of a morning early
Through black woods walking

     (Weave laurel with rushes
      Weave willow, weave broom)

"Comes bear, comes wolf
Deer and horse come walking

     (Make a crown full of feathers
      Dye mustard, dye blue)

"Come bear, come wolf
Lie beside me in the morning

     Come deer, come horse
     Till my body comes new"

One

In her sleep she grew wings, but when her father stood by her bed
she was a crumb of cheese

He had feathers dark as a corridor   they walked together   she could fit in his beak

till he dropped her
into a secret place

        one fly
        whispered with its legs

She did not want to cry so she counted
           on her nose
           outhouse smells:

                ammonia
                nectarine
                or some other
                      softening thing

Then her nose said, Welcome
           this is the smell I make
           warm straw, salt

She opened her legs   her father   held light on a stick   she closed her legs

Now her feet knew the path back to the house

                her bed was a sky
                      she would fly

                        till morning

All around the island
Dance up dance down
Dance till the stars fall
To make you a crown

Dance till you're silly
Dance till your head
Knows everything and how to sing
Your baby brother dead

Mr. and Mrs. went out one night
Dressed in satin and silver light
When the party ended they strutted home
There was their little girl sucking on a bone

Heavens, said Father
Wipe your chin, said Mother
You're supposed to be sleeping
Like your good little brother

Sing beesting, gnatbite
Stupid stub-your-toe
Sleep in a crib where only
Babies go

All around the island
Dance up dance down
Dance till the stars fall
To make you a crown

Queen of the lightning
Queen of the sky
Watch the ocean shiver
As it rolls by

Ring around the island
Make the beach plum burn
Make the edges shrivel
Like an egg you turn

Snakeskin beetlecreep
Cricketwing crow
Nothing above me
Everything below

(No one above me
 Everyone below
 When winter eats my fingers
 Where do I go?)

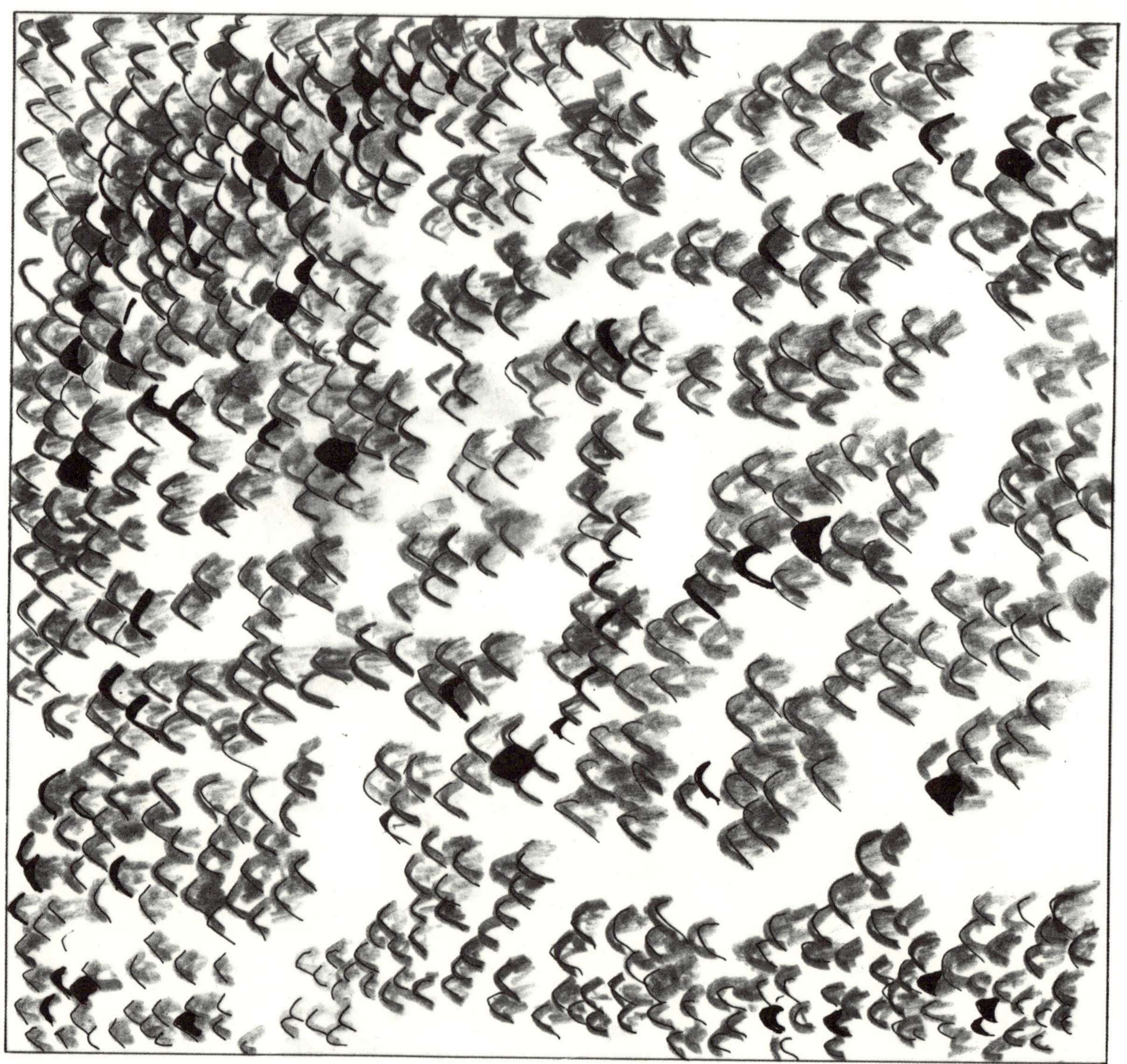

They were bringing sandwiches, white and brown, and a knife, and lemonade yellow and cold though it would get warm with pale splinters floating, and the baby's bottle and little jars. She was a fish in her shiny skin, the water curled and she tasted salt with her nose and waist, the quick waves slipped into all her holes. Her father spread his hands out flat where her stomach had no bones and she floated, her mother on the sand found a starfish for her to keep, her mother caught the sun in her lap, come and eat, she said. When her father opened the biggest bottle the red top leaped in his hand and the lemonade splashed, it went everywhere and didn't taste good, Jesus, he said, why do you screw it on so tight you're always doing that. Cut it out, she said, can't we even have a god-damn picnic.

O inside me

                a little pea

My stomach shrivels

                a little brown pea

My head goes with it

                silly peanut silly bee

little wrinkle little baby

                is me is me

"Where are you going Miss

                Dilly Down Dilly?

Where do you wander Miss

                Barleyseed Brain?

Where are you going Miss

                Dillyseed Silly?"

Down the path to the water
Down the little red lane

Met a hen there Mommy
She fed me lies

                (Miss Sillypea Sally
                  Miss Twist-up-my-face)

Met a rooster there Daddy
He pecked out my eyes

                (Miss Diaperwet Dolly
                  Miss Whimperweed Cries)

When the fight was over
They set my eyes to bake
Turned them into raisins
And stuck them in a cake

I am being eaten
                    (Come Mommy Come Daddy)

By a rooster by a hen
                    (Was I naughty? Am I bad?)

I am raisin I am clove
I am lentil I am prune
I have no flesh
Am bone   am moon

In the sky at night
                    (Black skillet black eye)

Two birdies fight
                    (Mommy Daddy O my)

And peck out the light.

Whenever she found the gate open, she walked through. The cows were used to her and if they stirred at all moved as slowly as bells, huge and bronze through the August heat. Sometimes she carried a basket of light-colored straw, but if she didn't have it with her she knew her arms would hold everything she gathered. Bending, she picked chicory, goldenrod, butter-and-eggs. There was more than enough to fill the wide-mouthed jug in the hall. Her daughter would be pleased, and her grand-daughter would laugh and ask if there'd be extra chicory; she liked to twist the stems into a wreath and play princess in a long cotton skirt.

Her own skirt was wrinkled from her walk but she would fold it carefully on a hanger. Lately she had found a quick nap in mid-afternoon gave her the strength she needed in the evening, for the cooking and cleaning-up and talking. She didn't need to sleep but only feel the weight of her body on the mattress, how comfortably the bed held her large bones. Simply closing her eyes made a difference, and she liked to imagine a new hat. It would be the color of wheat and she would cover it with roses, gardenias, morning glory — not worrying that they would fade, or whether the colors clashed. How extravagant, and how they would whisper when she wore it to church next winter.

• • •

Though the mornings were dark, she continued to take her showers cold. There was something helpful in the sting of the water, as if it could propel her out of her dreams into this world she lived in most of the time now. Thinking only of objects made it easier, the rubber grip on the handles of the wheelchair as she pushed him from the bedroom into the kitchen. Still if she thought of spoons she would remember the scraps of yolk and white in his bowl, how when she guided the spoon toward his mouth their eyes persisted in meeting. It was simpler if she tried not to think of him as one she loved.

Once her granddaughter had been in the bathroom and said how brave she was, all that cold before sunrise, but it wasn't that; it was standing in the shower thinking about her lips pursed over straight-pins. In a dream she was making herself a hat with tiger lilies and snapdragons, something foreign and close-fitting a gypsy might wear by a campfire. Or instead of hemming a dress she might have been born a bird with a quick sharp beak. Peck. Peck. Her husband was dying of a sickness that turned his body gray.

Peck. Peck. Out of the ice of the morning she rose on flame-colored wings, soaring above the town and the quiet land beyond. It was no longer winter. In her beak she held three matches and dropped their red tips into the fields. The long grasses crackled as the animals ran, mice, rabbits, toads and once she heard a killdeer call, its needle cry through brushfire, where do we run.

Two

Dream of a woman, hooded, who has the power to command dogs

Striding, striding

out of the pine forest
her skirts teem

these are the tents we dwelled in
before speech, in the smoke and fur

paintings on the walls of the cave crying
with desperate colors

        antelope
        peccary
        deer

           feed us your sweet, quiet smells

Whenever she sings, dogs

from the savannahs of blood and rabbits

             turn

               twelve tails thrashing

In a waking dream I sleep,

eat,
sleep

in the hollow where the rabbits shiver
in December
                Old woman
what did you bring me from across the ocean?

eat,
sleep

silver fish and oranges
she gives me
in a bowl

she can make fire
she can make snow
go away   she can come back

eat,
sleep

in the hollow
with the young rabbits where did you
take my tongue old woman?

sleep,
eat

in the morning
we nudge and sniff, our small teeth
gleam

24

Waking, I know the house. This is the room without clocks. All morning the closet holds darkness in pools quiet as after rainfall, night folded in sleeves and pleats. The robe is always hanging here, where my mother left it when she married, and the quilted peonies breathe in and out, tongue-colored, porous.

Long hall, chill and shadowy between bedroom and back stairs; I am glad for this robe that holds my body without question or constraint. The steps twist downward, angular, unreliable as snakecoil, this is the way to the kitchen where my grandmother does not feed me — I have slept long after her breakfast — but I find or make what I need.

She is moving through the rooms in the awkward rhythm of housework, stoop, straighten, reach to the mantel a soft cloth. Singing, a wordless alto tune, strong thread to draw her bones along from task to task. In the kitchen, when she is done, she asks me to come with her to the attic when I have finished my coffee, this would be a good time.

There is a room in shadow and a room in light. It is the back room I know best, where the trees behind the house keep sunlight filtered and tame, away from the trunks heavy with wedding gowns and shawls. The front room, stark and brilliant, faces the street without protection; she walks easily here past books stacked shoulder-high, ant hills, ancient and precarious.

"I want you to have this book when I die," she lifts it from a carton and the birds fly up, from a volume of old prints, wings flash ruby, indigo, steel, I want you to have this, hummingbird, egret, hawk, to have this dove, sparrow and thrush and jay, mockingbird, kingfisher, teal, I want you to have this, wren, falcon, whippoorwill, take this heron.

Three

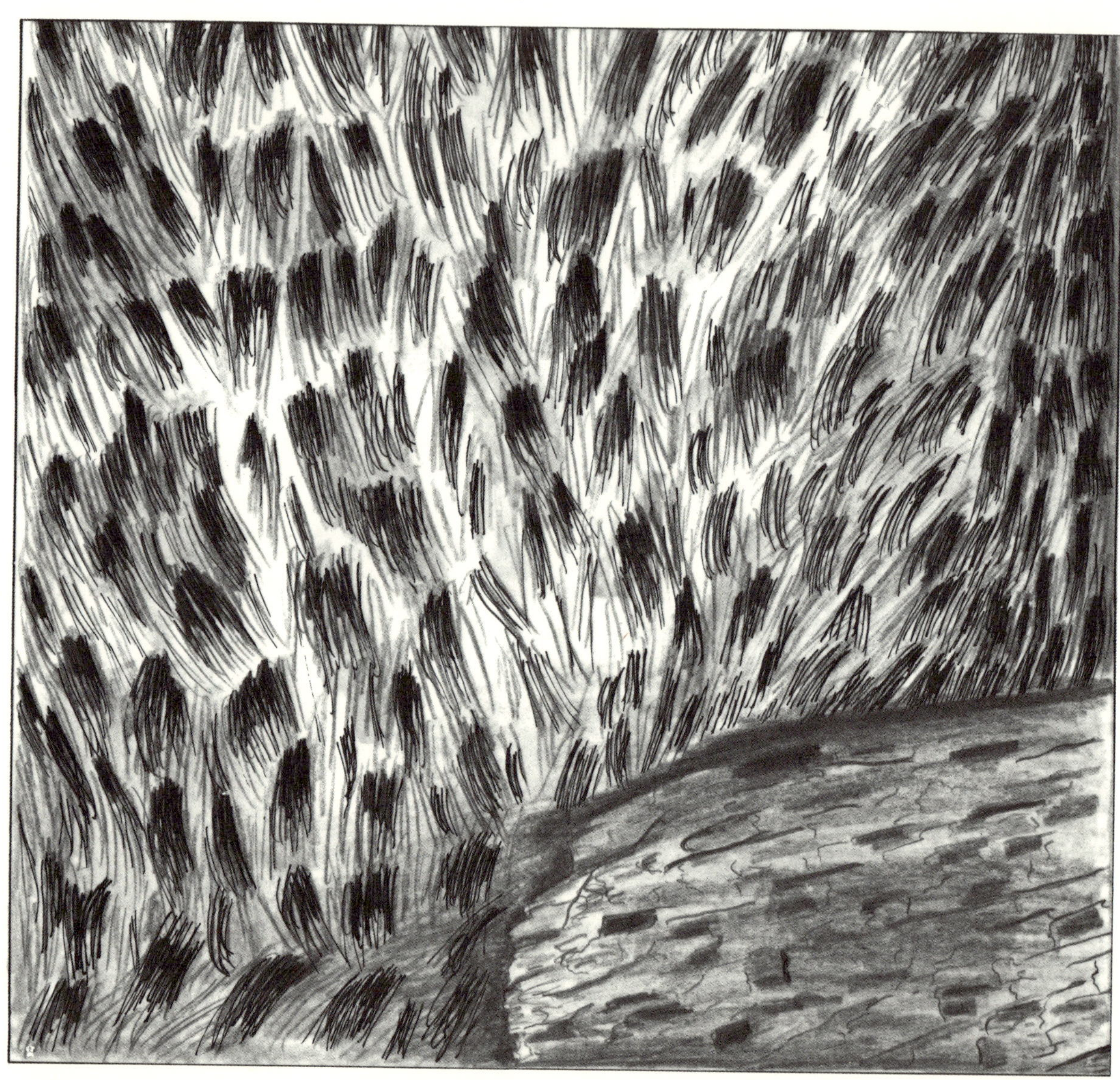

For a long time I could not understand the sudden weight I carried in my body,
as if some animal had settled inside me into an endless, troubled sleep. This was a
mammal with thick bones and tiny, stupid eyes, struggling like a tree sloth to survive
on land. It must have fattened recently on insects scraped from the underside of a
log; some of them clung to the fur near its mouth where the strands stiffened.
Breathing, one night I heard its breath echo in the dark, and a smell drifting — faint,
the pastel of eggshells or bananas — up from the warm sponge of the lungs. Even in
sleep it probed with the moist, clumsy ruthlessness of a snail, slipping at last to my
throat as to a green stem. We breathed together now, unison, a simple song.
Nothing to hear but the rhythm of my sleep, or what the snail attends to, pulling its
shell steadily forward as froth swells behind on the trail, on the long leaf of the iris
where bubbles glint and splinter.

I could tell this story another way. Late in November I noticed a change in my body. It was as if my stomach suddenly refused to digest, so that although I ate no more than before I felt bloated, weighted down. Supper sat like a lump of biscuit unchanged inside me; I ate breakfast as a habit, not a need or want. One evening I let suppertime pass, resolved to wait till my hunger returned. The next morning I woke up empty, and discovered overnight I had lost ten pounds.

I was surprised, but not worried. I felt supple and light. To avoid feeling bloated I began to eat smaller portions, and as I was rarely hungry at noon I worked straight through the day. Yet the heaviness returned to my stomach, fattening on smaller and smaller meals. Dessert shrank from an apple, to half an apple, to a quarter. Day after day I was hungry only for supper. Early in January I lost another ten pounds in the night.

I was puzzled, and finally afraid. I felt my clothes billow around me. I began to talk with doctors, to give blood for tests. Now I weighed ninety-eight pounds. There was nothing wrong with my body, how was my mind, they asked. I am happy, I told them. My work is going well and I live with a man I love. I am happy.

When rain woke me I lay for a long time listening, until drops dissolved roof and blankets and seeped through my skin. A quiet invasion, the sentry drowsy before sunrise, banners of the enemy colorless, ragged as fog. Am I going to die, where am I going? Quickly I rose and dressed. "Enough self-pity," I told myself. "If anyone's dying it's Grandma. Think about her."

She had fallen, months before, in her kitchen. Unable to stand, she pulled herself to the phone. No one could say how long her hands lay flat on the linoleum, how many minutes or hours her voice lumped fierce and cold in her throat, refusing the wheeze, the scalding syllables, I need, I need. The doctors removed a tumor pressing at the base of her spine. Yet there was a second growth, invisible now, which would swell from a pinprick to kill her. There was no way of knowing when, five months or five years.

The phone rang the next morning at six. Grandma died easily, my mother told me, in her sleep that night. We were thankful she hadn't lingered in pain, but I cried with the ache of missing her. It was two years before that I had last seen her in Connecticut, though we wrote often and called several times.

When I found the bed again in the dark, Bob held me and told me his dream. He was watching television when the program was interrupted by a news bulletin. Someone had died, and he was sure it was someone he knew. He couldn't see who it was because I was sitting between him and the screen. Get out of the way, he kept saying, Judy get out of the way.

We talked for a while and then tried to sleep. I miss her, I cried to myself, this is for the best but I miss her. Behind my eyes a cord joined temple to temple. It grew taut, then thickened into a knot pulsing in my head. The knot ached, but I was tired and stumbled finally into sleep.

●　●　●

Make a fist. Press each nail into the pad of your palm. Harder. This grief traded its voice for a snare drum. Tighter. When the skin cracks, as the sheath of your lips shrivels in the desert, you will no longer be able to cry. Rattle instead, rasp at the tip of a snake's tail, or curled in the fingers of a baby.

Since you cannot speak, you look carefully. Beneath sleep your eyes are wide. Now you slip into them like water and they receive you, this ocean is deep and knows no drowning. Buoyant, you let your fingers float loose from your grip, your fist remembers its birth and blossoms, anemone, your hand makes a cup and you bend to drink.

Milk on your tongue, whales in this sea and they nurse you, gray against your mouth, whiteness sweet in your throat. Drink. Sleep. Drink from the whale your mother your grandmother, feasting, this milk flows, archipelago of women, rustle of waves against islands, the bright smooth sand, your own breasts listen, grow full.

32

Sun in the room when I woke, and the knot had loosened behind my eyes. In its place swam slow, easy circles of dream, fish slipping through coral and weeds. It is all right, though I will miss her it is all right.

Hunger took me then by surprise, an enormous room without furniture. Suddenly my body held unexpected corners, echoes and polished floors. On my back under the blankets I stretched my legs to the edge of aching, each muscle strong and extended, welcomed, called by name. Toe. Ankle. Calf. Knee. So much space, how should it be filled? Slowly, deft as a painter I began to imagine breakfast, fruit and cereal in a bowl, sugar, milk. Or I could begin with apple, red or green or yellow, the skin simple and luminous as in a child's alphabet book. Banana, a yellow arc flecked with brown or black. Three dark cherries, three stems joined at the tip.

Or I would run through the vault of a station in winter, hips jolted as feet slapped concrete, each breath torn on the jagged air. A train pulled closer, slowed down, I ran harder, panting, shoved my way through the thick stubborn bodies of the crowd. From the platform my eyes opened wide in greeting: colors flashed at the windows, shapes in quick bright patches. A scarf grew long with squares, blue wool white wool blue wool white wool. The glint of a zipper, red galoshes, somebody's wrist. Sparked by hunger, I rejoined the world.

Dress, take the dog outside. A clear cool morning. Camellias the color of a hummingbird's throat. My knees feel weak, almost buckle, I stagger like a toddler, learn to walk again. Upstairs awkwardly into the kitchen, reach for the radio dial. Music leaps out, fast piano, fastest recording ever made. The announcer's proud voice. He smiles. I eat Grape Nuts, milk, sugar, a banana, orange juice, toast, margarine, coffee.

Through the day my mind returned to her death, simple as a tongue over teeth. I could not find her. Still there was a strange exhilaration, something in the quiet of her death that tipped a clean light across the world. Undeniable that I felt joy. Carelessly it fed on whatever was at hand, harmonica or the smell of eucalyptus, a boiled potato. The next morning I discovered I had gained six pounds.

In my mind I held the past months carefully, remembering dreams, my mother's phone calls and my grandmother's short, scratched postcards. My hunger continued, and though I gained only four more pounds I knew my body would hold firm this time. Somewhere in the night my grandmother died, my stomach had sloughed off its sullen weight. My grandmother's pain had started, my mother told me, near the time my stomach had first grown heavy. Yet I had not known of her illness or even of her hospitalization till my parents called a week later. There was a link, I thought, between my body and her body, some unseen cord of grieving, anger and sustenance that ran below the surface of these months. Floating, belly flat on the sea's rim, if I peered and peered I could detect the shape of meaning, wavering, vulnerable, distant as an embryo, far under water.

Near a lake in the hills above Oakland Bob found a bench where we could sit. He drew a letter from the pocket of his parka: "Your mother asked me to give you this." Her words were fish scales, glistening, edges sharp against evasion. "I would like to be with you to tell you what I have to write, but you should know — it will help me to have you know — that Grandma chose to end her life with an extra dose of sleeping pills."

Alone in the hospital, her body motionless under bandages and metal, she shaved her Protestant faith bone-clean, and fierce as a minister's daughter called law and custom and pain by their rightful names. "I believe in God and life after death" — in a note left on her desk the night she died — and earlier, to my mother, she spoke of "useless pain." "Useless pain": again, on a pad between grocery lists and phone numbers, where in columns *pro* and *con* she weighed the reasons, her need, ours; ethics and money and God, children and grandchildren. Moved to the country, at the rehabilitation hospital she looked from her wheelchair to snowfields, snow and fields and trees and sky stripped stark to white and black, a core without excess, luminous, surviving.

Stronger — "wheelchair-independent," the hospital said with demonic cheer — she returned late in February to the house she had lived in since her marriage. My mother knew she was getting better when she began once again to make plans: Mrs. Pierce would come for sherry, my brother would come from Michigan on his vacation the week after. It was he who explained what my mother could not at first find words for. "She did what she wanted to do, death didn't cheat her," he said when he heard later how Grandma died, sleeping her way beyond pain or affection, pulling her weathered body, with each long breath, on oars steadily farther from shore.

I take this ritual because it is what I know. You will know others, and there are many none of us knows but may discover with quiet and luck. In the church I was raised in, at the end of the week before Easter, all candles are one by one extinguished till a single candle stays burning, behind or under the altar. The church lies in darkness, an empty field. My grandmother died on Ash Wednesday, some thirty days ago, but now in this week before Easter, which I have not celebrated for years and will not celebrate now, I choose this time to return to her dying.

Miss Patterson, the gentle, rigorous woman who taught me Latin in high school, taught me also a medieval hymn, the Stabat Mater: the mother was standing, we translated, grieving at the foot of the cross. In the eighteenth century Pergolesi set the hymn to music, a piece for soprano and alto which Miss Patterson played for our class, itchy in navy blue jumpers, the morning before spring vacation. Now I take out my old record and listen as the voices interweave, low and high, back and forth, oldest of lullabies, women singing low and high, back and forth about death.

When Mary's son was taken down from the cross the women brought spices to anoint the body. What can I find in my kitchen, what shall I bring for an offering? On the Saturday before Easter I scrub the oven, shower, bake bread with saffron and currants. I spend part of Easter at the laundromat, and driving across the city to find a fish store that is open: I want to cook fish with lemon for supper. Also I drive to another store to buy flowers, purple and yellow and white iris, which I put in jars and old bottles all around the apartment. The errands make me tired and a little irritable; I have almost forgotten Grandma by late afternoon when at last I can sit.

I come downstairs and outside to the creek that runs, mysteriously in mid-city, below the old frame house. Today is no different from other days and the creek is clogged with garbage, a mattress and a shopping cart and an empty can of yellow paint. But there is always water that trickles through, down from the hills to the bay, and blackberry bushes with lush leaves and thick, efficient thorns. I sit in the yard on a patch of grass. I am very hungry and have brought a glass of white wine, cheese and a cracker. I need to eat, to think about my grandmother and then not to think, to live my life again simply, without the impediment of death or mystery. I am tired. I want whole weeks of the ordinary.

I have white wine and cheese and a cracker because I am hungry, and because I remember drinking and eating these things with my grandmother two years before, when we would sit in her house and talk before supper, and turn on the news when it was time. Before I go upstairs to cook supper I eat and drink and close my eyes — I am not sure why — for a moment's imagining. My grandmother stands in her kitchen, whistling an old hymn, looking through the window to the yard where a bird sings on a hawthorn branch. She is wiping the table after breakfast when in an instant she disappears. Now she is a bird singing on a hawthorn branch in the yard. Now she is a bird flying so quickly I can scarcely follow, and when the bird leaves the range of my sight I am thrust once more, living, into the secular world.

Four

As it was evening and her father was visiting the house, she lit the long white candles. Will they fall, shall I use them, do we have others. All through the meal, her wondering. Her father was a careful man.

As a girl once at supper, just to see, she had held her napkin in the candle flame and for a single sweet instant watched the paper flap and roar. What are you doing? they cried and sent her upstairs to her room. They were right and she didn't sulk or mind the hole in her stomach, only held carefully in memory that blazing second of grace before the shouts and danger.

In sleep her arms were slow to recognize their load, light as a bracelet of shells felt only when the wrist trembles. Was it shadow or wind — or else this fear circling her pores like an insect at dusk — that made her arms stiffen, grow still?

She was holding their child, not yet conceived and so almost weightless. It was April in her dream, and everywhere pale blue. She understood the child as a bird's nest of twigs and shredded paper, with sometimes a curl of ribbon, silver or white. She understood the nest's vulnerability, now and for a while to come, as night stalked and twittered around her. Still the baby's cheek against her breast startled her with its softness, inescapable: she woke lonely, with a knowledge of danger.

• • •

She wanted him to wait here, in this well-lighted room. There were plants hung from the ceiling. Someone had opened a book to a painting by Matisse: he remembered the woman's hips, the puff of her Mediterranean hair above the earlobes. He was drinking white vermouth with lemon. Though he wanted to be with her and their child, in her dream she kept him away. He was sitting on a wicker chair. In the room next door, he imagined he heard her crying.

• • •

She cried softly, not wanting to wake the baby but she felt helpless. What could she do to protect her from even a common childhood illness, the fear of nightfall shading her stomach with a prickly rash? Or later, after breakfast on a hot July morning, what if suddenly there were a telegram? What could she do? What could he do?

• • •

It was dark in the room where he waited, the woman in the painting had dis-
appeared and there were no colors. He could not see into the room next door or
even imagine its walls and furniture, or her body and the body of their child. If he
were to fall asleep and then awake and stumble in on his way to the bathroom, he
could become at any moment a dangerous man. It would be easy for him to bump
into her, holding their baby in the darkness. He would hear the rap of an egg against
the rim of a steel bowl. His heart would swell and turn yellow and slip like a yolk
from between his ribs. At that moment the child would vanish, they would feel her
vanish like a snail underfoot. They would each stand there in that darkness, helpless
in striped pajamas, waiting for someone to bring a glass of milk and a cracker.

Archipelago

Where the herring runs I run far from the island
where eyes of the herring float stunned
as clouds where the anchovy flashes, stiletto I go
where the sardine shivers far
from the island the beachplum is burning the children
are gone on the beaches the gulls drop
fire from their mouths the white waves sizzle fieldsnakes twist
in their skins toads turn pellets of earthcrust popping three mice
blinded flames slice the long grass three tails curling the field grows

nails on its fingers the sky sheds
slivers of moon where do I run
when the squid's ink darkens
this cold star-swallowing
                              sea?
                         Old breaker old chip-
toothed woman old saltweed belcher I slip
through my bones I dissolve without spine I am
egg of the sturgeon I jelly I blacken these waters
teem with me myriad mother of
black and seed, mother of green and wandering
plankton, mother of stars, sealilies, rustling
milk in these waters, mother of whales
mother of serpents
eddies and worms
wheel and rim
spin and spark

            swirling, swirling far from the island, rustle of waves against

other islands archipelago milkbright sand death makes the surface
gleam this cup must I also drink this milk floats
teeth and tongue away ice in my throat thin finger lingering
gullet to toe this cup must I also?

(this and this and
yes and this and)

mother of sorrows stay with me
now in the hour of my
mother of sorrows stay with us
now in the hour of our

floating, sea between islands links us
wave to wave our bodies smoothed
between sea and sky sloops, we are more
than one procession milk the winding
cord that draws us smoothed between folds
of shoreline glistening after rain we are more
than one we are more
than many bearing
gifts in the hold of our bodies, winding
flotilla of colors and fruits, winding
flotilla of beasts and seasons these our gifts
from world to world we take
this ritual these our bodies:

ebony
amarillo
brown with its deepening weather
whiteness of shame and angels:

here our dwelling

apricot
papaya
plum ripening grief-blue
melon that swallowed a moon:

here our dwelling

jackal
gazelle
lizard light as shadow
panther who eats flesh by night:

here our dwelling

hurricane
snowdust
August stained with berries
autumn polishes cold teeth:

here our dwelling

Sloops
fragrant as spruce or mountain
glide between islands

our cargo quickly
a feast for moths or air

slowly

    see how we rise, sails billowing
    over the sea we are huge

        birds calling, each to each
        our cries persistent, raw

    I need, I need

        lovely without end or answer

photo by Robert Fitzgerald

Judith Small was born in San Francisco and grew up in New Jersey. She earned degrees at Oberlin College, Harvard University and San Francisco State University. She has taught high school and college, and now works as a legal assistant in San Francisco. Her poems and essays have appeared in *Poetry Northwest, The Massachusetts Review, New Letters, The Chariton Review, Big Moon, Room* and other magazines, as well as in the anthology, *From Shadows Emerging,* published by Black Oyster Press in 1981. She has been the recipient of a Fulbright Fellowship, the Fels Award of the Co-ordinating Council of Literary Magazines, the *Poetry Northwest* Young Poet's Prize, and the San Francisco Browning Society Award.